Also by Anselm Hollo

GUESTS OF SPACE

Guests of Space

Anselm Hollo

COFFEE HOUSE PRESS
MINNEAPOLIS

Coffee House Press books are available to the trade through our primary distributor, Consortium Book Sales & Distribution, 1045 Westgate Drive, Saint Paul, MN 55114. For personal orders, catalogs, or other information, write to: Coffee House Press, 27 North Fourth Street, Suite 400, Minneapolis, MN 55401.

Coffee House Press is a nonprofit literary publishing house. Support from private foundations, corporate giving programs, government programs, and generous individuals helps make the publication of our books possible. We gratefully acknowledge their support in detail in the back of this book.

Good books are brewing at coffeehousepress.org

LIBRARY OF CONGRESS
CATALOGING-IN-PUBLICATION DATA
Hollo, Anselm.
Guests of space : poems / by Anselm Hollo.
p. cm.
ISBN-13: 978-1-56689-192-9 (alk. paper)
ISBN-10: 1-56689-192-2 (alk. paper)
I. Title.
PR6015.O415G84 2006
821'.914—DC22
2006012063

FIRST EDITION | FIRST PRINTING
1 3 5 7 9 8 6 4 2
Printed in the United States

ACKNOWLEDGMENTS
Some of these works have appeared in *Art Paper* (Boulder), *Bombay Gin, Big Bridge, call: review, canwehaveourballback, Chicago Review, Conjunctions, Den Del's Devil's Gate Auto Repair, Fayetteville City Poetry Review, Interim, Jacket, Melancholy Breakfast, Murmur, Paper Tiger, Shiny, Sniper Logic, Snout, Square One, Sulfur, Ur-Vox, Yolanda,* and in the chapbooks *A Bit of Hades* (left hand series), *Ancient Land Animal* (Big Bridge e-chapbooks), *Anon: The Continualist Anthology* (Potato Clock Editions), *So the Ants Made It to the Cat Food* (Samizdat Editions), *The Guy in the Little Room* (The Dozens). The author is grateful to the editors, publishers, printers, and distributors of these publications.

To Janey
and all our artist and poet friends

Contents

So the Ants Made It to the Cat Food

THE GUY IN THE LITTLE ROOM

SUCH AN EXPENSIVE DREAM

GUESTS OF SPACE

GUESTS OF SPACE I

Guten Tag Herr Schopenhauer Bonjour Monsieur Cioran
good morning Mr. Swift how are you Mr. Burroughs
once again history the unstoppable proves you right
species no better than smart rat (maybe not even as smart)
evolutionary leap? my foot, my foot in three-foot hole
but let all peaceful mutants leap for spring
calloo callay, while they still may—
watch it! don't twist that ankle!
don't step into that three-foot hole!
"and wisdom has not come" "against wisdom as such"
oh, it is apt to give a gopher tantrums!
anecdotal befuddlement. infinite terminators.
toujours a mountain eased a previous you;
should it feel easier, writing? I don't think so. No.

"and wisdom has not come": "Wisdom has not come, says Pollagoras. Speech
keeps strangling itself, but wisdom has not come." —Henri Michaux, *The Old
Age of Pollagoras* (trl. by Laura Wright). "against wisdom as such" —Charles
Olson, in *Against Wisdom as Such*, pp. 260—264, *Collected Prose:* "I take it that
wisdom, like style, is the man—that it is not extricable in any sort of a state-
ment of itself . . . " "gopher tantrums" —minor "Ghost Tantras."

here have I summed my sighs, playing cards with the dead
in a broke-down shack on the old memory banks
e'en though my thoughts like hounds
pursue me through swift speedy time
feathered with flying hours
but could have sat there for many more hours
listened to poet friends reading
words by an absent friend whose work we love
in the name of Annah the Allmaiziful,
the Everliving, the bringer of plurabilities
concretized, concertized, temporally minute
progressions of actions, swirling mists of the past
"you have a lot of stuff here, you know?"
"yes   now run on home"

"here have I summed my sighs": Samuel Daniel, *Delia:* Sonnet 1. "e'en though
my thoughts like hounds": conflated lines from *Delia,* Sonnets v and xxxiv.
"in the name of Annah": James Joyce, *Finnegans Wake.*

Once you've said something, you can't unsay it
Once you haven't said anything, it remains unsaid
and anything you can't say, well, it's unsayable
All right now that we got that out of the way
we need some particulars
but where did I put them, where are my particulars?
"Here they are, sir." Oh, thanks. Today's mail:
3 books of poems, 1 cigar catalogue
the poems look great, so does the catalogue
"But aren't you trying to quit?"
Mel Tormé died, Charismatic didn't make it today
the fifth of June nineteen-ninety-nine
And in a restaurant called The Europa Ninety-three
warlords consult on a respite from murder and mayhem

"in a restaurant called. . .": Located on the border between Macedonia and Kosovo, the "Europa" was *bought* by NATO for a meeting between Yugoslav and NATO military commanders.

i.m. Hannes Hollo, 1959–1999

Fought the hungry ghosts here on Earth
"What is man?" asked the King
Alcuin's reply: "A guest of space."   And time yes time:
The past lies before us, the future comes up from behind
Walking on Primrose Hill or Isle of Wight beaches
Iowa City streets scrambling up snow-covered deer track
To Doc Holliday's grave in Glenwood Springs
His helmet now shall make a hive for bees
He fought the hungry ghosts here on Earth
Strong & resourceful on his best days,
Patient kind and *presente*
Returning those with him to here & now
But just as we settle in with our Pepsi and popcorn
THE END rolls up   too soon   always too soon

"'What is man?' asked the King": Pippin, son of Charlemagne, 9th century
C.E. "His helmet now . . .": George Peele, *Polyhymnia.*

and of course it won't do, it won't do at all
Herzen again: "Suffering inescapable,
infallible knowledge
neither attainable nor needed"
sound of swans' wings
over the quarry ponds at Grez
look up! the departed sail on
to some picture-book Norway
and Mr. P old ga-ga cantor
among the ruins of Europe
writes to his missus "where are they?
where are they?"   old "genius" snows falling
on his head in his head
(no, it won't do, it won't do at all)

"Herzen again" —Aleksandr Herzen (1812–70), Russian revolutionary thinker
and writer, "the one with heart in his name."

Private they are, the sums of grief, "impossibly private"
"There probably is some intelligence at work here"
"Yes, but I don't want to know what it is"
Elizabethans considered a nosebleed a symptom of love
But if'n the wind don't blow through it   it don't make it
& what if the 'personal' prove as tiresome as the 'public'?
Mawkish messages to the dear departed? No
That is not given to you to do
Nor can you really get behind idealized forebears
Getting wiped out while attacking some barn
"Did you say *barn?*" In the glorious South or any other
Cardinal direction. & now this old Cardinal
(Universal Life Church) hums
Cani capilli mei compedes   "Gray hairs are my chains"

Against meaning, lunatic, real,
Possible in appearance, you work a line,
Be like a larger logic to defy
The dumbly trembling unities
(quotation fringe is blue)
Your self helps us from prose & down
Into an orange: "Hail my effort, you people"
"Stand and deliver!"
But stubborn world is time & airy dung
Insists on legible distance, inhabited heaps
"As Lacan points out"
Never mind what Never mind Never mind
Sing the old huddles (persons bowed down
With age or heavy wraps

& should I buy this *Scientific American*
to see how the quest for immortality is going?
got the one on space exploration
. . . such incredible hardships ahead . . .
calling twenty-nine-ninety-nine in this old English
but we are just learning to walk
and time is a voice goes a-roaming
"just a chickadee in the rain"
Green House almost ready now
oh they too have their troubles
the belovéd intuitive abstract expressive painter
the ever-distracted monkish poet
musing upon the Malevich square on Hitler's upper lip
and the fact that "questo" does not mean "quest"

the human being talks it talks
and talks and talks   even to
itself   so "hating speech" what was
that about? no speak no talk no read no write
now *that* sounds like the dead except
some of them do read them-
      selves into our ears
day and night
      when The Slinger passed on
      it left me restless
      the way one was restless
      after a teenage rendezvous
"driving somewhere, fast
with the windows rolled down"

"so 'hating speech'" —a reference to Robert Grenier's notorious statement "I hate speech." "driving somewhere, fast": my daughter Tamsin's memory of Edward Dorn, from when she was 5 years old.

"would that it were otherwyse"

one eyebrow raised
Sir Thomas listens to his quill

(check Wyatt quote) (can't find,
it's not a Wyatt quote) (so what,
it's you   trying to sound like him)

o would that it were otherwyse
friends did not have to die

Andrei Voznesensky, in Iowa:

"TRAH-DZHED-DEE OV ARTIS
EEZZ: ARTIS HAFF TO *DIE*"

bye-bye Fielding
bye-bye
Falstaffian
fun

Fielding —Fielding Dawson, master of USAmerican poetic prose: 1930–2001.

I'll write a poem about nothing
absolutely nothing
not about myself
or youth or love or any person
I'll write it riding along
half asleep in the sun
and then I'll send it to a friend
signed, William of Aquitaine
nine hundred years ago
and ever since we've raged
in shirts red black and blue
we've raged still do
in our dream rooms asking the air
mad questions about nothing

The Duke of Poitou's poem can be found on page 7 of Paul Blackburn's
Proensa: An Anthology of Troubadour Poetry. For the shirts, see Ted Berrigan's
The Sonnets.

Equipped with human heart's dizzy gyroscope
In the yellow submarine we lived oh my darlings
Is it now all just imaging?
No more *imagining*   in The Momentous Events
In Small Rooms Hotel   the brain is?
"Don't remember the time I was born
Don't want to remember the time I die"
Old troll stands in secret memory garden
Gazes at mirror globe's beloved faces
Through time they move as "guests of space"
Yes that we are he thinks remembers Alcuin's answer
When Pippin son of Carolus asked him "what is man"
& Cousin Louis: "You will always do wrong
You must try to get used to that, my son"

"human heart's dizzy gyroscope" —Tristan Tzara, *Poem for a Dress Designed by Madame Sonia Delaunay.* "Old troll" —"Moomin Papa" in Tove Jansson's great *Moomintroll Saga.* "Cousin Louis" —Robert Louis Stevenson.

My first computer:
Poor old workhorse machine
Just an advanced version of the clay tablet
Archaic box, you still work
Humming that hum I found so irritating
22 years ago
       (used to say "this thing's
          no smarter than an amoeba")
Waiting for me to write
A word and then another
And another
But I shouldn't have said what I said just then
Because only a few days later
It went from hum to loud groan   And died

There's words, and there's hair
And hair and hair . . . Would you know
Evocative if you saw it?
Or have you not had the Enigma
Reversal Experience?
"What's that?   What's that?"
They cringe and snarl
It has to do with the minutely sensational
Say I, with what's little enough but enough
As when you turn the radio on
And it is the right music
Even when It introduces sadness
And one understands little
Of what's going on

and thus we woo our wit with gentle memoranda
birthday thoughts about mother long gone
& her madcap cocaine-addled sister
Aunt Karin I never knew, her son cousin Peter
ever wistful but such a smile   now gone too
dusk road games   dust road fumes
REALITY is WET today
"How big is the mind?
How could we avoid dissolving
in our own private oceans?"
asks Randolph Healy dear Irish poet
beat, beat   "It's a strange, strange world we live in,
Captain Jack" and who was that and why
(look up at the sky, bro, look up at the sky)

"(look up at the sky, bro, . . ." —Allen Ginsberg's recommendation for states of
mild depression.

all that fifties-style
wretchedly splendid
better living through chemistry
when people said things
like "haven't I seen you somewhere before"
always worried about hitting exactly wrong note
hence tall strung-out conversations
with hypothetically beautiful persons
remember those? but now
I am pissed off at you old sport
even though you are dead
to my regret & possibly even yours
no longer hanging on to tatters of poetic mantle
or moth-eaten unacknowledged legislator's wig

Addressed to no one in particular; a composite (possibly even self-) "portrait."

You
      are not the Countess of Tripoli
And I
      am not dead yet
                  unlike Jaufre Rudel
So now I can tell you about
The most interesting metrics of The Horse
To wit, the *rack*, the *fox trot*, the *amble*
Four-beat gaits with each beat
Evenly spaced gliding and smooth
In perfect cadence and rapid succession
The legs on either side move together
The hind leg striking the ground
Slightly before the foreleg!
                Vraiment,
Poetry can be so many more things
Than what people mostly believe it is.

And there were years when nobody died.

"Countess of Tripoli," "Jaufre Rudel" — "Jaufre Rudel [. . .] fell in love with the countess of Tripoli without ever having seen her [. . .] because of his desire to see her, he took the cross and put to sea. He took sick on board the vessel, and at Tripoli they thought he was dead and carried him to an inn. When it was known to the countess, she came to him, to his bed, and took him in her arms. [. . .] Then he died in her arms." —Paul Blackburn, *Proensa.*

GUESTS OF SPACE II

When in a mood of fair-
Ground music mortality   Drift
Down Feral Boulevard
Wearing your sentimental formal
To the bar called "The Far"
Sit down to a think
I won't be back
You won't be back
He She It won't
Nor will We You They
In the Twenty-First's air
And none of them
Will ever want to hear
From whom they haven't heard *of*

make big fat sounds
list the two or more places
where you'd like to be
at once and more than once
where questioning every question
hasn't killed all questions
(at least not yet)
and all is long damp hedgehog love
on a perennial sunny tourist morning
then go there ASAP
and send me a postcard
that postcard will be this poem
wish you were there already
wish I was here

perhaps we exist
as the notes of the string exist

back when all was continuous chuckles
a trembling fringe of cryptonyms
hermetics winking in the magic tree
sweet as Bizet's *Fair Maid of Perth*
ah but those lovely *hoarse* 15th century horns
(now it's cool again to be "passionate")
old man thunder rolling o'er the hills tonight
the open window full of logic you tell yourself
that via this literality
you may recover a semblance of body
"certain things happen
 & continue, they exist in us
by a species of recurrence,
 they fall   vividly   into our days & nights"

Epigraph and last four lines from Ezra Pound's *A Walking Tour in Southern France* (ed. Richard Sieburth).

from up there on the ridge
the successful manufacturer of vacuum cleaners
surveys the valley: ah,
all those little lights—
each one of them a "home"
with at least one of
his dear machines!
it is festive
it is the festival of Saint Retail
that ends every good u.s. American's year—
martinis über alles!
but bellicose poem no buy dinner
but the sea slug remembers everything, you hear?
It remembers   Everything

"but the sea slug" —sea slugs have been immensely helpful to human memory
and dopamine receptor research.

Now that was pretty simple-minded wasn't it.
A dog barks in the dark. It's simple-minded.
It probably belongs to some simple-minded person
who cannot understand what the dog wants. The dog wants
some simple-minded attention,
that's all it wants.   2. ~~So softly stirs~~
3. So stubborn are the boots
walking an old man. His matter hesitates
where there are doors among the glaciers
furred with brine. O softly stirs, when he goes out,
the next-door cat, pees on the holy book
under his pillow. So the old guy grits his teeth
and wishes for that song "She Is a Country Woman"
to call him back to the bars of? Late Modernism?

What's current? I mean misheard?
Currently misheard? Shelf dancing? Alpine badminton?
Now write a sampling on one leg
Of composed being with shaky eyelids
Who tells you "I am in the art, but molecular
Only by dint of a visiting pillow;

                      I am the author of *Author.*"
Now shall we agree, say I, before the bar is toothpicks
That poetry is a chicken   in good mud-tennis weather?
Such tube-lit discourse. Ten dollars a waltz.
No tidy archery. So sell me that bumper, no, I meant
The mouse calliope, yes, that's it! The ego
Seriously in tears at the holy beneath
Dangerous furry feelings—beware the hole punch
Of darkness, shrunk from the world.

                   So. One mouse calliope, please.

In this world of snickering squirrels
Who gives a hoot for Jesus in a box
Or was it his brother? the one not begot
By Zeus. One much prefers
Even the obvious, but if you must be obvious
Keep it brief—with maybe a witty touch.
Lissen, lemme tellya sumpn, says Lemmy
Caution, the tough guy of many French movies
I don't give a rat's ass if you don't
Think that's funny. You don't think that's funny?
Them squirrels sure think it's funny.
He sure was a caution, that Lemmy,
He was. And an Italian mile is a thousand paces,
So is a verst on Mother Russia's roads.

Lemmy Caution —Runyonesque character in pulp novels by British author Peter
Cheyney. French filmmakers based a number of thrillers on Cheyney's books, with
craggy Algerian-French actor Eddie Constantine as Lemmy, who also appeared (as
Lemmy) in Jean-Luc Godard's *Alphaville.*

Past middle-aged, I enjoy the Middle Ages (some-
what) in Visby, Gotland. In Visby, Gotland
in the Baltic Center for Writers and Translators
the fire alarm goes off three times a night
without fail. A brace of Mormon missionaries describes
their Utah religion to a group of Medieval Swedes
one of whom wants to know "But where IS this AMERICA?"
Jane finds a sheet of paper in her night table drawer:
"Writers are at their best when they have no idea
what they are doing." It says this in Swedish,
attributes it to Nelson Algren (in Visby, Gotland).
Shouldershooting Duck: A Manual is a book
I find in Visby, Gotland but do not buy.
Be here now. Then be there, then. In Visby, Gotland.

"An ancient land animal" Man in wheelchair
comes rolling out of old folks' home
I hold the door open for him

He looks at me, says "WIND'S PICKIN' UP . . ."
rolls on down the slope to the parking lot

not heading for any car! but the good old Open Road
—I'm beginning to have my doubts

when a nurse comes charging after him
an air of disapproval about her

she turns him around and pushes . . .
I help her pull the chair back up the slope

They perform a successful reentry

"So a lot of time has passed   But without
the imagined future having come to pass"

"'An ancient land animal'" and "'So a lot of time . . . to pass'": Carla
Harryman, discussing the part of "Reptile" in her *Memory Play*. I was assigned
that part in a reading of the play one summer at Naropa in the nineties.

Bright sunny "garden" apartment
A euphemism for basement, like
The one in San Fran
Where late the L=A=N=G=U=A=G=E poets sang
But bigger bay
Window out to street
Sitting with someone in some
"Waiting excitement"
Big black limousine or hearse?
Pulls up, hey it's my mother
Amy!, elegant in black with black
Toque or perhaps medium-brimmed hat
Veil in back, gets out
We embrace, she (sort of) groans

my mother was not The Great Mother
your mother was not The Great Mother
even though they were pretty great
there were times when they were not so great
but they were just human beings
like you and me
and that goes for all The Great Fathers too
that said "a short discussion followed
during which Tony Lopez raised poignant questions"
but I wasn't there and I bet you weren't either
but in weird dreams
recumbent incoherence
our parental molecules   long dispersed
do make the odd return appearance

Glazed with alcohol, old sailor
Reels into me on Stockholm street—"Heyy, you old fucker!
How are ya! Remember the times in Veracruz?"
(And he is not "Stetson" and I am not T. S. Eliot)
What *would* you say to the ones you lost if they appeared
Before you as themselves, as who they *were,*
Not merely these phenotypes
That surface now and again in bodies, faces, in ways
They gaze back, mirror your own puzzled look?
Uh, welcome back? Long time no see? Where have you been,
And how? Or oh, it's been so long . . . But that
Is what those puzzled eyes do say
Before they turn back to the living
(Who needs to dwell more than half a second in Hades)

Tracking down some of the (now unreadable) books of my youth
Proves nonproductive   So now to get back to where
Fabulous meets Nebulous? But no they've booked passage
With ANT TRAVEL, INC.: an agency
Whose motto is IN DOG WE TRUST
& playing with fire when it burns Yeatsianly low no good

    "Don't have a home in this world any more"
    Some ways he never did have much of a one
    Mon fils but who am I
    To say what the world is

"What was it I just remembered?"
"The 10,000 little resentments"

Felt a little like crying   Or maybe burning a couch
Like some of the ignorant human spawn of this burg

They discussed the Code of the West
"Plan your moves   Pick your place
Don't make any threats   Don't walk away ever"
Enter in black fur coat
Mournful eccentric   Songs of lamentation
Evening at Donnelly's Pub in Iowa City
Thirty-plus years ago
"You look just like Frankenstein's Monster!"
What to do but grin back at him
With bad original teeth: "I AM HE!"
And this is way too literal
So hand me that drug of Egyptian origin
Mentioned in the *Odyssey*
Before the guys with the torches arrive

"They discussed . . ." —reference to a recurring line in Ted Berrigan's *The Sonnets*. "'Plan your moves . . .'" —text in a collage made by Ted and Alice Notley from the 1970s.

IT WAS ALL RIGHT
or, What I Learned from Kenneth Koch

It was all right to be funny   all possible kinds of funny
It was all right to be erudite
All right to use as many words of the English language
     as you could possibly come up with
All right to be elegant   all right to be rowdy
But never all right to be pompous
It was all right to be modern   and postmodern and premodern
All right to be all of those at the same time
All right to be for intelligence and kindness
     and against hypocrisy and dumb power
All right to believe in your wishes lies and dreams
All right to tell what you had never told anyone
All right to be a poet   a lover   a lover of words
All right   it was all right   thank you Kenneth
Thank you for *Thank You and Other Poems*
So many   other   poems

Hundreds of prisoners of the motor car
grind past this office window every minute.

A league is an hour's walk.
A lecture is an hour's talk.

A *li*—a hundredth of a day's march.
No one's counting but you.
And an uphill *li* is shorter
but takes longer
than a downhill *li*.

Millions are dying! Millions being born!
And here he sits worrying about his sick cat.
That's all right, Anselm,
says the central committee
of a million gods. We're counting you, too.

Traveling into the past on the Internet
I see an old friend from forty years ago
Now dead five years. He hasn't changed a bit.
Or listening to a tape there are lots of feathers
Another friend's feathery voice
Stilled in a mix of blood and French gasoline.
Deserters both of them, one from Hitler's army
The other from consensus reality:
"When he was good he was just mildly insane
When he was bad he was out of his mind"
& into another we could not know.
And this is one of those "long ago" poems.
They did give me courage: I still run
On some of their *essence*. They were fine *déserteurs*.

"essence" in French —gasoline. The friends: Anton Fuchs, Austrian novelist
and short story writer, 1920-1995. Piero Heliczer, American poet and
filmmaker, 1937-1993.

On the tenth of March, two thousand and three
      Bix Beiderbecke
would have been a hundred years old
just like
      Carl Rakosi,
            then still alive.

Did Carl and I ever listen
            to Hector Berlioz?
I do remember
       listening to the *Symphonie Fantastique*
with Gregory Corso, up in his little room
with a view of London's Primrose Hill
where Sylvia Plath walked with her young . . .

"Time is a great teacher,"
          said Hector Berlioz,
"but unfortunately
       it kills all its pupils."

So the Ants Made It to the Cat Food

now that some of the young ones
have taken to writing
like Eugene Jolas and Elsa von Freytag again
(if not quite as vigorously)
(pass the thesaurus, said the dinosaurus)
we may once again enjoy the "oh I see
(s)he just found out about that" experience
ready for the impending product
besieged by books looks at a book:
"this I have read" looks at another:
"this I should read"   picks a book off a pile
"now where in the hell did this come from?"
memory browser stumped   old owl
just a slip of a girl

"Eugene Jolas and Elsa von Freytag-Loringhoven" —early 20th century avant-
gardists; see Jerome Rothenberg's anthology *Revolution of the Word* and biog-
raphies of William Carlos Williams.

cannon goes boom boom   canon goes round and round
every decoding's another encoding
& when the teachings haven't
quite   sunk in . . . it may be quite interesting
but could be more interesting
just isn't interesting enough
"admired, he lets his work
warp back into itself
for this, he admires himself"
but where is she? what happened to herself?
then there's the awkwardly dwarfish
sculpture of Mr. Robert Frost
in front of Colorado's "Old Main"
slung a little too low for pigeons to shit on

lives deaths "A Life"
three days with A Life
of one who painted meticulous magic
in 1930s Paris, Antibes
great c l a r i t a s more than in anyone's cantos
. . . rough seas lately but . . . "I can hear birdies". . .
now Rudy's gone to join Edwin in death pond
old Hem one hundred
he steeled my heart for heartbreak
cursor flicks across screen
"shut your eyes hard
against the recollection of your sins
do not be afraid
you will not be able to forget them"

"three days with 'A Life'" —Amanda Vaill's biography of Gerald and Sarah
Murphy. "now Rudy's gone" —Rudy Burckhardt; "Edwin" —Edwin
Denby. "old Hem" —Ernest Hemingway. "'shut your eyes hard . . .'"
—R. L. Stevenson.

....rue Blue
where we stopt between rattling journeys
.....................................noon street people
...................like seaweed mocks the water
......................................glide swirl oratorio
.......................in the world's pretty pinions
.............................long company of time
............"and the Cristo came back as a fly
with a million eyes" ....
daylight crackles ....behold the garden
pale record of selves................................
....just an asterisk
....this is an asterisk
(example of asterisk)...............................

"Successions of words so agreeable"
Yes they are yes they are
So agreeable successions of words are agreeable
& a great deal of it all was Greek at first
Before it was Roman the way it still is
Ah the simplicity of those lives
Oh no there are no simple lives
So many hours per place
So many ladders of grief
Now is this all about the great themes as listed:
Death! Truth! Meaning of Life!
Love! Romanticism! Loss! Reality! Consciousness!
Symptoms of universe we be
And we pray for an end to idiocy

"'Successions of words are so agreeable'" —Gertrude Stein. "great themes as listed" —on Gale Research poetry web site. "Symptoms of universe" —Alan Watts: "We are the symptoms of the universe."

"The range of cultural & historical reference
& information in the mass and popular media
is remarkably limited"
French popular writers have a thing
about fucking on top of motorcycles:
the beast with 2 backs
doing a hundred and twenty
But I am just learning to talk
"How could we avoid dissolving
in our own private oceans?"
Life squiggles on
perchance to leave a record forlorn
private impossibly private
(I thought it was Red Bug Dermatitis)

"'The range of . . .'" and "'How could we avoid . . .'" —USAmerican poet
Charles Bernstein and Irish poet Randolph Healy in e-mail tertulias. Tertulia
—Spanish for regular, informal, literary, or artistic gathering. Last parentheti-
cal line refers to the scribe's case of shingles.

Why am I reading this ill-written tome
About the lousy life of a 19th century hoodlum
With a big knife? Because
It just might help me understand
A particular strain of USAmericano "mentality"
That resists Evolution
Tooth and Nail   Handgun and Literal Bible
(irritable parenthesis: big knife too messy now)
The Protocols of Elders of WASP
But now to think of a better subject
Irwin Catullus who passed away
Three years ago to this day
He cultivated a different strain, the one
That brought me here   To be a guest of this space

"a 19th century hoodlum" —Jim Bowie. "Irwin Catullus" —Allen Ginsberg; "to
this day" —April 5 (1997).

inkling   in/kling   ink/ling
Norse "enkel" equals single equals simple
Middle Dutch "enckelinge"—a falling or
          diminishing of notes
Middle English a whisper, a murmur, low speaking
a hint, an intimation
                    "To inkle the truth"
actual instance of speech
years lost in the alleys of making
minimal unities of meaning
possible in a line
Eluard: the Earth is blue like an orange
& I'm just a tepid heart inhabiting The Blossom
with tactful terrorism. The tear-stained screed

Things people say
"I think you're a very lonely man" said one
Another one said her friend said
"He's just a sentimental lumberjack"
I must have reminded her of Jack Kouack
Sentimental sí Lumberjack NO
More like a jolly garden gnome
And as for lonely no I don't think so
More like lonesome which is American
As American as applejack by the quart
A favorite among Iowa Writers' Workshop
Lumberjacks   A dead or dying breed
Can't believe I am saying these things
People say   These things, these things

so the ants made it to the cat food
but then you scrape them into the compost

one day we'll set out under solar sail
to the systems of fifty new planets
discovered this year

who knows if we'll do any better
than these ants you think
then contemplate vast grids upon grids
shifting and twisting
clashing and jelling flowing apart exploding

shrinking   to this little blob of cat food
in the kitchen sink

oh it gives one the flesh of the hen
comme on dit en français.   cat disappears into bush

"comme on dit en français" —as they say in French.

PRODUCING UNSALEABLE FOR . . .

HOW DEE DO . . .

THAT POETRY'S SMART TWADDLE MY MAN

LE PARADIS N'EST PAS ARTIFICIEL

PRETTY LOT. DO A THERE.

SO ABOUT, OR THEY THEN?

WELL SHE PRETTY, AND OF

IS. WE MODERN,

PREMODERN. THE THE. WHAT'S THE DIFF?

SELF-RIGHTEOUS ASSHOLES

BENT ON THEIR POWER & THAT.

OF THEIR HIDEOUS OFFSPRING.

ALL CAMPS. HELL ARTIFICIAL TOO

ON LITTUL BOOL.

"le paradis n'est pas artificiel" (Fr.) —"paradise is not artificial": Ezra Pound, in
response to Baudelaire's *Les paradis artificiels*. "bool" —boule (Fr.) —ball
(globe). This is a "treated graffito" sonnet.

All of last year's farewells
in this Piranesi
parking lot
"Seems we can't get to the right level"
"Hope to see you again"
Bye-bye Haa Tsay Aytch See Art Man
"Vissi d'arte, vissi d'amore"
Whence this Italian that keeps creeping in?
Old Ez? Joe C? Piero? old bones
remember young bones now old, too
have lived for art and lived for love
how many to a pillow sprouting wings? en la memoria
He sure was one funny monocle
a living breathing *House of Usher* played as high comedy

"Bye-bye Haa Tsay . . ." —H. C. Artmann, the postmodern Austrian trouba-
dour, wit, bon vivant, great terrible lovable guy, d. 2000 c.e. The last two lines
refer to him, as well.

      & then we went
Alice and Doug and Jane and Anselm
(small sample of us featherless bipeds
who measure conscious existence in paltry decades)
to have some diner at the old inn
with its sign to inform us that Victor Hugo
had "descended" there   for a night or two

And that was only a little more
than two turns around the sun

                       ago   ago
And the gods have slain many since then
and so have the people
                 Yes, so have the people
the riders of the purple rage

"History always written by the victors"
(Confederacy sure disproved that adage)

"to have some diner" —"diner" to be pronounced in French,
approximately "diné."

this is not the bear this is a picture of the bear
's big head   stunned then deleted

newspaper story: Old Grizzly "Falls Creek Male"
aged 22 years   for 15 of those avoided traps
outsmarted humans killed dozens of cattle
"worth up to a total of $200,000"
finally trapped given lethal injection
April 18 in Bozeman Montana

he did not know that those cattle were MEANT for food
for humans who couldn't kill a cow if they tried
were MEANT to send the rancher's kids to "college"
were MEANT to perpetuate one of stupidest cultures
        ever constructed on this planet

this is not the bear this is a picture of the bear

Speech balloon above head reads "Does poetry help?"
The answer to that is only if you can turn your head
Three hundred and sixty degrees, then turn it
Faster and faster, so it becomes a fuzzy blur—
In other words, if you're an owl! But you're not an owl,
You're a person. Persons need house,
But persons need persons more. "SHUT UP DOG!"
Who was that? He's right. Ah, life:
"Sometimes I see it as a straightforward
Linear equation
Drawled with a pendant and a rumen
Transfiguring the circulation of the worm."
That was a quote from our new Poet Laureate,
Somewhat improved by "seven up or down."

"'seven up or down'" —Oulipian method of replacing nouns in an existing text by
other nouns occurring in a dictionary "seven up or down" from the original ones.

THE GUY IN
THE LITTLE ROOM

In the back of your mind is this little room, and in that lit-
tle room is this guy, and that guy, if you read lots of poems
all the time, that guy will learn everything about poetry,
about form, and shape, and when you make your poems, that
guy will take care of all the technical details. All you have to
do is write those poems. But that guy, you got to feed that
guy plenty of material all the time, or else that guy will start
raising a giant ruckus in the back of your head, and you'll
think you're going crazy. It's only because you're not keep-
ing that guy busy, you know. And that's true — believe me.

— TED BERRIGAN

So now   they have pressed
Their singular gods into service again
"A pillar of fire by night   A pillar of smoke by day"
Twenty-four hours before that massacre
In the city garden not far away
I saw that wing-lamed crow
Pursued by the landlady's sweet-faced cat
Shooed it away and the bird
Managed to flap over the wall
Into the garden next door where Ted Berrigan
Composed a "Poem Written in the Traditional Manner"
Forty years ago: "I summon
To myself sad silent thoughts,
Opulent, sinister, and cold."

So it's a return engagement between
The Short-Sighted Corporate Greed Heads
& The Nothing-to-Lose Religious Fanatics

Unbridled capitalism
Versus "adolescent disease
Of humankind" (Arthur C. Clarke)

"The days of fun and waste are over"
"Someone has hanged himself in a rectangular emptiness"

Yes people are scary
People who fall in love with a singular god
Are really scary
50 million dead in World War Two
The end of honorable warriordom
If ever there was such a thing (10 million in WWI)

now that the empire done struck back
how come everybody's feeling like merde
head full of rubble is that a metaphor no
sounds like a headache to me
statuesque angel drifts by how nice but no
it is hauling a banner that says
NO IDEAS BUT IN HAMBURGERS!
should one pretend to be very pained
when one is simply fed up and grouchy
"there is some shit i will not eat"
yes that's a quote oh boy I used to wonder
how anyone could end up looking
like winston churchill
but he was an angel

compared to these neo-beowolves
yes evil is live spelled backwards, by dog
is that him over there
waving his hefty defense budget
"fat free! flat rate!" stop cluttering my mind!
was that the author yes he just left the room
was it the obvious author yes
with expensive precision weapons
to defeat the enemies
we need more of
like we need more of more itself
unless we can manage
to be ousted from the joust
of pawns against pawns

When you're feeling
about as
bad as your
average

English translation
of Goethe you must
go see the
Parrot of Penance

and he will
say unto you
"Way around it?
Way around it?

There's never been any
way around it"

what are your daily inspiration needs
(you don't know that you know that)
but childhood's insect musketeers
as they thrust parried danced
on those transparent pages
they sure were fun
their authors wrote
to please their champions
and made you feel like a champ
hegemonic   mildly imperialist
but you didn't know those words then
nor did those authors
but nothing will ever take you back
to a place   a time   a child

feel like evil spirit
ride the black horse wear the black hat
regret just about every thing
be a good boy be a good boy
regret just about every other thing
once in a while rejoin the human club
with a touch of the whip a shot in the arm
be Siegfried ice cube old cold fish
dream a little dream with me
cat woman bird woman
faint whiff of extended family
long ago far away   so love
where are you marauding tonight
in the vast bog of terminology?

Would it be sentimental to state
That the wild apple tree's red blossoms
Give me shivers of joy?
Well, have you ever heard
A mountain lion burp?
Sort of abruptly?
Me neither
But now, on the digitized didjeridoo
We have The Dolly Lama
Who deserves a big hand
Unlike the poet who writes things
Like "the air's faithful oblong"
Assignment: Look at these lines
Again in a hundred years

By the end of the day
I will have said all
I had to say
This day   to loved ones
Friends associates grocery checkout persons

And quietly   in my head
Even to those little gangsters
In their sentimental suits
Who run the show

And seem very fond of
The Kiplingesque expression
"At the end of the day" (harrumph)

Trying to indicate that they just know
What something they call The Outcome will be

SUCH AN
EXPENSIVE DREAM

first they asked for your *Ausweis*
then they took you to Auschwitz   Kosovo! Kosovo!
the way the species now does what it does
is the way it has always done it
& the way the species will do what it will do
will probably be the way it is doing it now
exactly the way it has always been doing it
Kosovo! Kosovo! yes, the species: a serious underachiever
may well go on flunking Conflict Resolution 101
until the end of time
in the great continuous absolutely unstoppable
weave of sad memories medium of human existence
"a murderous dream, confetti falling
helplessly into the fissured past"

March 7, 1999

Ausweis (German): "identity" card (or "papers"). "'a murderous dream. . .'":
from Rachel Loden's poem "Premillennial Tristesse" in her book *Hotel
Imperium.*

because our lives were so short
we had to imagine One more patient than we
perhaps even one reborn every year
so we celebrate the man who reenacted Osiris
"cherchez la femme" yes quite possibly Mary
of Egypt   upon whom the Roman Empire
did *not* build its monotheistic monolith
& the zealots are of course always with us
the poor miserable and vicious zealots
Palm Sunday. Kosovo. NATO. Clinton
now tries to atone for Andrew Jackson?
stop Milosevic's Trail of Tears?
(after the innocent and the ugly
here comes the *bewildered* "American")

March 8, 1999

"(after the innocent. . ." —now, in 2007, it looks like we're back to the ugly, all right.

old "red" years now quite forever over?
along with postwar lyricism & doggéd cynicism
some breathless absinthe
some invigorating celluloid
much theoretical hovering above baleful
phantom formulations   poignant drunken lies
the ephemeral the recurrent the eternal
"Good Lord, if our civilization
could sober up for a couple of days
it would die on the third day from remorse"
the tribes are back in old cutthroat mode
freed from the yoke of Pax Communista free
to hunt among stones
to count the bones among stones

March 12, 1999

"the ephemeral . . .": E.P's whilom "plan" for the *Cantos.* "'Good Lord, if . . .'":
Malcolm Lowry, quoted by Albanian poet Genci Mucollari in e-mail from
Tirana April 1, 99. "to hunt among stones": Charles Olson, "The Kingfishers":
"I hunt among stones."

Now Cormac has sent word: "To all the lands
of civilization, beset by barbarians and by war,
bring us your books and works of art.
We will keep them safe in Hibernia
until the danger has passed—
even if it takes centuries!
From palaces and monasteries
the treasures have come—
first a trickle, soon a flood
Word of mouth was once our ally.
Now it is our enemy. Corsairs prey upon our ships.
All they want is gold and silver
to melt it down. The books
they throw overboard. We must have help."

This was the news from *Prince Valiant,* Sunday October 23, 1999. I started fol-
lowing his adventures 60 years ago.

"A strong tendency toward silence
. . . the poem holds its ground on its own margin"
Says Paul Celan   Yes, even if only in elegies
Addressed to our previous selves
On the troubles of The Naturally Immoderate
That persist even after you have become Moderate
Cut to dogs at banquet dressed up as people
Card I was going to send to my sister a decade ago
She gone now, shrunk away, into another dimension
But the cartels and monopolies still mutate and grow
Oil-slick amoebas over a universe they wish to appropriate
Thunk go the rubber bullets through hissing tear gas
While delegates snooze at long tables
In December's Seattle convention hall

"Thunk go the rubber bullets" —fired by riot police at demonstrators in Seattle
protesting the policies of the World Trade Organization, early December 1999.

The bread was cardboard
The circuses simulacra on a screen
In hilaritas tristis, in tristia hilaris

Strange to see our moneyed classes dressing up
As ants   so they can resent the impecunious
(Nay, "improvident" in their book) grasshoppers

The question arises out of the bubbling
Pot of questions (note: I do not call it a "cauldron")
The question arises why do I bother to write
These things
                    But so does the question why
Taxes we pay are used to finance slaughter
Slaughter and waste instead of hugs embraces
Friendly arguments about birds identified
Or even better   misidentified

                    "Oh man did you see that toucan"

"In hilaritas tristis, in tristia hilaris" (Latin): "Sad in gladness, glad in sadness"
   —Giordano Bruno.

If we could miniaturize
Our species

To prairie dog size
We'd be much better off

Never met a prairie dog I didn't like
Even though they can't read or write

They live in big cities
And they have "coteries"

Which means
They're good at setting boundaries

Unlike their present overfed co-inhabitants
Of the United States of America

Who let themselves be ruled by a gang
Of vicious thieves

if it's not propaganda, what is it?
if it's not brainwashing, what is it?
if it's not a capitalist oligarchy, what is it?
this ain't funny   not funny enough
how to stay funny enough
let's just go out and die
under the stars in the snow
driven by these little molecules
are you asleep are you alone
life a Riemann bottle
can't get in can't get out
but the music does tinkle on
driven by these little molecules
"see what you got, tomorrow"

Suits for the dead
Lawsuits for the dead
In war world's whirlpool
        sluggish explosions
      hope apathy whine roar

"I mean, how many vases do they have in there?"
Rumsfeld, "drawing laughter from reporters"

      "We live under a system by which the many
        are exploited by the few
        and war is the ultimate sanction
        of that exploitation" said Harold Laski

Written while recreating a death
      attended to over the telephone

Ah, America   Such an expensive dream

Rumsfeld —21st century u.s. warlord, commenting on the looting of Iraq's
national museum. Harold Joseph Laski (1893–1950), British Labour democrat.

Ah, America   Such an expensive dream

"My dream a crumpled horn"

    Listen to the wind

To keep the peace, prepare for war
    say the warlords

Little melodious raptures no help
    & war creates
                more warlords

So here you sit
    Dear micro-speck of star dust

To keep the peace, prepare for war

And who, among
    these throngs of deaf souls
        would care to hear
            your cry

"'my dream. . .'": a line from Ted Berrigan's *The Sonnets*, possibly borrowed from Conrad Aiken. Last four lines paraphrase Rilke.

mule deer fawns
cavorting in the backyard
backyard paid for
fawns a bonus

imperial president
cavorting on the deck of expensive killing vessel
paid for by you and me
president   no bonus

young humans dying
in a country occupied
to the tune of millions of dollars a day
paid for   by you and me

"mit der dummheit kämpfen die götter selbst vergebens"
"with stupidity even the gods struggle in vain"

Ah, to be a "National Poet"
wouldn't that be fun?

No I don't think so
They shot the last one
In the nineteenth century

& even less so
In the twenty-first
Where "spectacle overcomes thought"

& Xtianity so-called
's a perversion
Of the renegade rebbe's teachings

Shock & awe   Shlock & dread

Into the valleys of idiocy
They ride, our lords

for Harris Schiff

Boots on a treadmill   "Do not lean on this wall
It is not secured to the floor"
Do not lean on this heart
It is not secured to the brain   Boots on a treadmill
Well, here comes another book of poems . . .
What are the findings?   Boots on a treadmill
Stagger on yes bloody well stagger on
George Orwell's four motives for writing:
Sheer Egotism   Aesthetic Enthusiasm   Historical Impulse
The desire to record things as they are
For posterity   & last but not least
Political Purpose—the desire to push the world
In a certain direction
Stagger on yes bloody well stagger on

COLOPHON

Guests of Space was designed at Coffee House Press, in the historic warehouse district of downtown Minneapolis. The text is set in Caslon.

FUNDER ACKNOWLEDGMENTS

Coffee House Press is an independent nonprofit literary publisher. Our books are made possible through the generous support of grants and gifts from many foundations, corporate giving programs, individuals, and through state and federal support. Coffee House Press receives general operating support from the Minnesota State Arts Board, through an appropriation by the Minnesota State Legislature and from the National Endowment for the Arts, a federal agency. Coffee House receives major funding from the McKnight Foundation, and from Target. Coffee House also receives significant support from: an anonymous donor; the Elmer and Eleanor Andersen Foundation; the Buuck Family Foundation; the Patrick and Aimee Butler Family Foundation; the Foundation for Contemporary Arts; Gary Fink; Stephen and Isabel Keating; the Lenfesty Family Foundation; Rebecca Rand; the law firm of Schwegman, Lundberg, Woessner & Kluth, P.A.; the James R. Thorpe Foundation; the Archie D. and Bertha H. Walker Foundation; Thompson West; the Woessner Freeman Family Foundation; Wood-Rill Foundation; and many other generous individual donors.

This activity is made possible in part by a grant from the Minnesota State Arts Board, through an appropriation by the Minnesota State Legislature and a grant from the National Endowment for the Arts.

MINNESOTA
STATE ARTS BOARD

TARGET.

To you and our many readers across the country, we send our thanks for your continuing support.

Good books are brewing at coffeehousepress.org